Pointers to Reality

Reality

A Collection of Insights

or Spiritual Transcendence

Zahra Publications

SHAYKH FADHLALLA HAERI

Published by Zahra Publications
PO Box 50764
Wierda Park 0149
Centurion
South Africa
email info@sfhfoundation.com
www.sfhfoundation.com
www.zahrapublications.com

ISBN: 978-1-928329-17-6

Contents

About the Author

Born in Karbala, Iraq, Shaykh Fadhlalla Haeri, comes from several generations of religious and spiritual leaders. After several years living and working in the west, he rediscovered the universal relevance of the Qur'an and Islamic teachings for our present day. His emphasis has been on transformative worship and refinement of conduct, as preludes to the realisation of the prevalence of Divine grace. He considers that the purpose of life is to know and resonate with the eternal essence of the one and only Lifegiver - Allah.

Introduction

Bismillah

Consciousness is the cosmic mystery that provides all the ingredients to the majesty and beauty of Life and Existence on earth. We take the simple day-to-day awareness of this Life for granted, without the respect that it deserves. Every life moves towards higher and higher levels of consciousness, often a great source of delight for us, when we witness the distinctions of growth in awareness of this beauty. Glimmers of Awakening provides some helpful reminders to us that our direction is always towards full awakening, whether it occurs in this life, or in the next.

I hope that these aphorisms will give you the sparks of delight of our purpose of life.

Shaykh Fadhlalla Haeri

Acknowledgements

The author would like to acknowledge the following people: Ahmed Baasith Sheriff, Zaheer Adam, Hasnayn Ebrahim, Aliyah Haeri, Hussein Haeri, Muneera Haeri, Muna Bilgrami, Leyya Kalla and Zaheer Cassim for their assistance in bringing this booklet to production.

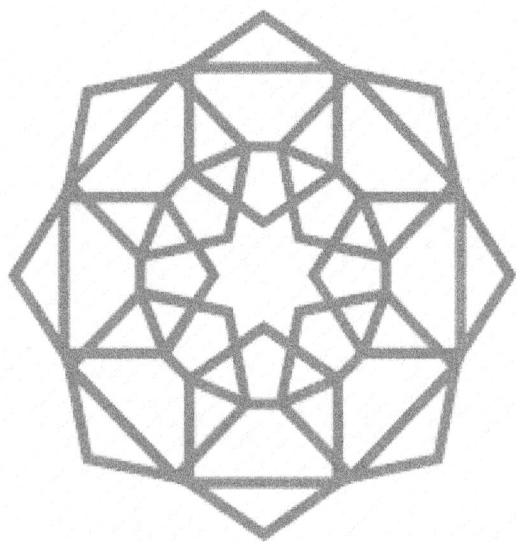

1. Life

The mystery of life and consciousness
is veiled by the illusion of individuality,
personal identity and the fantasy of free will.

In truth, all existence is a lie searching for its
origin: the Truth.

Life is sacred and eternal; every living
creature is obsessed with it.

The purpose of earthly life is to realise Life
itself — eternal and perfect.

Every living creature is obsessed with its life
and its preservation.

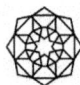

Life manifests as discernible experience,
energised by unseen forces, within a
timeframe.

Human life may seem short but life itself is
eternal and causes human life.

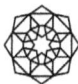

The obsession to prolong life simply reflects
the eternal nature of life.

Pain is the guardian of the continuity of life.

Love of life is accompanied by fear of death unless you are awakened to perpetual life.

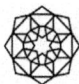

The body is alive due to the unconditional love of the soul, which connects it to life's source.

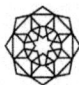

Living creatures love life and fear death. Few humans discover that the true nature of life itself is eternal.

To attain a complete and fulfilled life you
must be at one with your heavenly origin —
the soul within.

The desire to be useful is to experience
being able to act for a purpose. Life's overall
purpose is to realise the perfection of all that
exists and its governance.

Everything one does is essentially motivated
by the passionate obsession with life.

Human life's ultimate purpose is to complete
the seamless connectedness of the present
moment with timelessness.

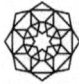

The natural universe is not silent or noisy.
It is in perfect turmoil and cycles of
interaction between matter and energies
— self-organising.

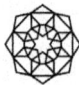

Plants are rooted in earth and nourished by
air, sun and sky; they are both earthly and
heavenly, as are all living creatures.

The full meaning and challenges of life are revealed through reflection and meditation.

Life is the greatest plot! In conscious life one quests for knowledge and appropriate action, yet the beginning and end of one's life are shrouded in the mystery of silence.

Intelligence facilitates the continuation of consciousness.

2. Humanity

Your opinion, prejudice and conditioned
consciousness are due to your humanity, and
your drive to go beyond the entrapment of
time and space is due to the light of divinity.

Living creatures are trapped by the
interactive qualities of attraction and
repulsion, diverse energy fields, and
numerous physical, chemical and biological
relationships.

Most human beings plan and act in ways
considered beneficial to them without
questioning or knowing who they really are.

Humans are naturally driven to addiction, irrespective of the habit being constructive or destructive. Intrinsically the self-ego is obsessed with its soul but is distracted and confused.

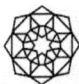

Humans are naturally driven toward conclusion, outcome, result, completion and the experience of the end of a project.

We are naturally curious about our surroundings. We want to know where does a road end and what is there on the other side of a hill.

To trust, have faith, or expect a better
future; to hope and believe in a loving God,
is part of human nature giving rise to desires
and needs for fulfilment, contentment and
happiness.

All human desires and hopes stem from
the one original drive to experience eternal
cosmic oneness.

To experience unity is a powerful driving
force in life. Marriage is a human attempt at
oneness at the physical, mental and spiritual
levels. Failures are balanced by success.

Full human potential is beyond human capacity to comprehend – it is the cosmic potential of the soul, the resident master of life.

Humanity's longing for the unknown is the prelude to being at one with the all-knowing soul.

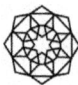

Two minds cannot always be fully in harmony, but souls always are.

Our normal consciousness is based upon our outer and inner sensations — this is nature. Then there is super-nature, containing intuition, insight and extrasensory perception, and then there is supra-nature, completely beyond mental discernment.

The consciousness of an infant is the mirror image of the very old, short-term memory as well as vagueness and uncertainty regarding all experiences.

Humanity is a manifestation of divinity and can lead to it, or darkness or light.

We love and seek justice in all situations
and whenever we cannot justify a thought
or action, we blame something or someone
else. The name often given is the lower self
or ego.

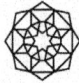

Much of human endeavour is shaped by
ambition for fame and fortune, avoidance
of failure, shame, loss of status, and / or
being accepted.

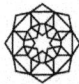

Human arrogance and vanity are countered
by nature's power of majesty and
unpredictability.

Humans survive and thrive due to a healthy
culture and communal co-operation.
Concern for others is a good remedy to lose
self-concern and focus on the soul.

Friendship and co-operation can easily turn
to competition and opposition when it
comes to material gain or loss.

The fear of being left alone will attract
others with a similar fear.

The highest level of humanity is found at
the door of divinity.

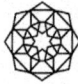

Humanity is an inspiration from divinity
and is darkened due to the illusion of its
independence.

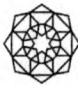

Intelligence is like a searchlight that enables
discoveries and insight at many levels.

3. Self and Soul

Every self is naturally ordinary and brought
to life by the extra-ordinary soul.

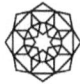

The ego-self evolves in consciousness,
reflecting the light of the soul and its higher
consciousness.

(The) Mind is an essential faculty for
survival and prolonging life but can become
an obstacle to arrival at the truth that Life is
perpetual.

Our self or mind is like a shadow of the divine on earth: the lesser the darkness, the clearer is the light.

The nature of mind is to seek certainty, which is mostly elusive, whereas the heart knows what is transient and what is permanent.

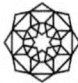

When the mind is agitated and the self is restless, the soul beams its perfect light unconditionally – always.

When your soul is discovered and acclaimed
as the master, the ego tries to sabotage and
reassert itself.

The nature of the connection of the self
with its physical manifestation, as well as the
extent of its unison with the soul determines
the state of the human.

The two constant voices within you – the
animal self and the higher self — often
mingle and cause confusion.

You have hoped to be someone else – in
truth, you are not who you think you are.

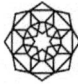

The desire to be approved is the hope to be
connected with life itself.

Life's experiences drive us to acceptance and
contentment in all situations. Our soul is
ever content and the self reflects its colour
and attributes.

Each human being is stable and constant as
well as changeable — that is the dynamic of
soul and self.

Whatever is visible or discernible is balanced
and rooted in what is invisible and unknown.

(The) Mind is the faculty that relates to
duality — to witness unity, you need to
transcend it.

The mind relates, measures and judges, and the heart reflects the truth that is beyond all mental activity.

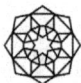

The mind seeks choices and the truth declares — there is no choice except perfection.

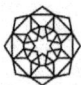

Optimism is part of human nature, so is pessimism. One is due to the light of the soul and the other is from the darkness of the self.

Loneliness is a message from the soul to
the ego-self saying, I am your soul mate,
be at one with me; thus, you will celebrate
solitude with a joyful attitude.

The pain of loneliness is the dark side of the
joy of solitude.

Quality life can be experienced when (the)
love of self is part of loving the soul — the
balance between selfishness and selflessness.

The root of all personality disorders is (a or the) lack of harmony between self-ego and soul.

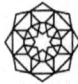

When you know yourself, the sacred soul and its shadow ego, you can tolerate others with deep understanding and compassion.

Prescriptions and outer actions are visible indications of subtler self-soul interactions.

When you know yourself, the sacred soul and its shadow ego, you can tolerate others with deep understanding and compassion.

Outer wealth and power conceal inner wealth and power. The self veils the soul.

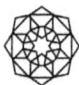

No one loves you more than yourself. Your soul loves you unconditionally.

The quest for the Holy Grail, the elixir of life, eternal youth, and other ideas are responses of the sacred light emitted from the soul and spirit.

The most valuable and amazing entity within any human being is the soul or spirit and everyone has the same gift.

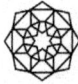

You think that you are dying but your soul never dies. One is you in transit, the other is perpetual light.

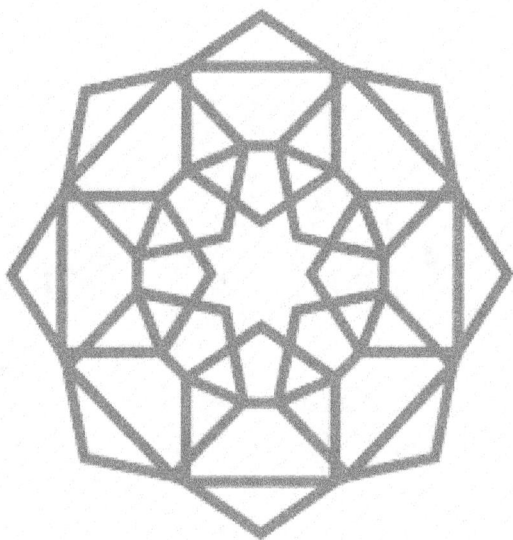

4. Two Zones of Consciousness

Truth becomes effulgent when conditioned consciousness yields to the light.

If you have an identity or roles, you are within the confinement of space and time — which you are always struggling to get out of. Your timeless reality is ever constant and boundless.

Our love for winning or receiving gifts and favours echoes the heavenly gift of the soul — the ultimate treasure; given with grace and unconditional love.

These are two maps for your life's journey:
one is for your earthly survival and describes
your body, mind and emotions; the other,
for arrival, and it describes your heavenly
state — inner soul, your heart and your
resident deity. These two zones do not mix
but complement each other. Read them both
side by side and you will enjoy your fate.

There are two types of poverty: the first
relates to outer needs and desires to reduce
human hunger and factors for survival and
the second is intrinsic — outer wealth may
not eradicate it, as the lower self is always in
need of the higher.

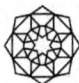

Is God in charge of everything or not?
Both! According to the lens of space-time
or Absolute Reality; this is the issue of
incomparability and similarity.

There are always two levels of successful
outcomes: one is as judged by facts, reason
and rationality; the other is to do with
eternally present perfection.

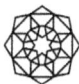

5. Evolutionary Drive

It is high intelligence to question the meaning of progress and development and where it leads to in so far as a fulfilled life is concerned.

Every decline or fall contributes to the future rise and evolvement of consciousness.

Human quest for freedom and liberation doesn't end except by awakening to the soul's light and its consciousness of the sacred present, beyond space and time and including all that there is within them.

We need stability, reliability, and constancy to awaken to the real and perpetual ever-present Truth.

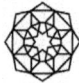

Money is power and we love its acquisition until we are at one with the most powerful source — the soul within.

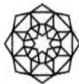

Easy success may easily lead to failure.

There is some goodness in being on a
direction, whether good or bad. There
is only confusion and loss in meandering
aimlessly in darkness.

Confidence points towards certainty without
dismissing uncertainty.

Uncertainty is constant and certain, always.

The gift of having choice may lead to the freedom of no choice.

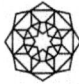

Every fact reveals an aspect of truth.

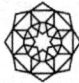

Every time is perfect.

The drive for contentment and happiness
points toward higher consciousness.

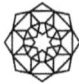

Self-expression is energised by the soul's
grace to help with rise in consciousness.

Self-preservation is a mere reflection of the
truth that life is perpetual and eternal.

We are indebted to generosity and the ultimate indebtedness is to the source of all generosities — God.

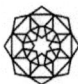

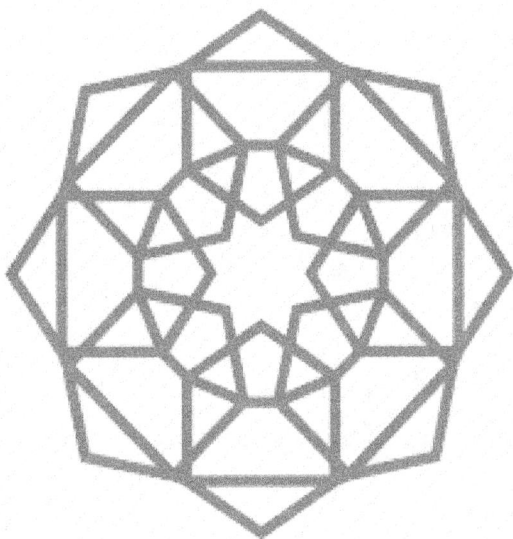

6. Revolutionary Drive

Safety from self-concern and anxieties is the fruit of reducing the suffering and needs of others.

You will have less personal sorrow and regrets when your concern is to help others in need of help.

Our drive and hope to satisfy desires and needs is to have peace and tranquility, which is a desirable and attainable state when the mind and heart are free from desires, fears and attachments.

A good actor knows the author's intention
and plays the role with head and heart to
fulfill the author's purpose.

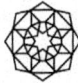

Desires never end, so what is it that may
give you everlasting contentment and joy?

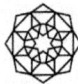

Ignorance is a handicap and deficiency.
Knowledge is power and responsibility.

Attempting to prove or disprove God's existence diverts from the drive towards higher consciousness and the original cosmic light.

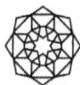

Truth is eternal and a lie only lives briefly as allowed by Truth.

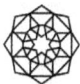

To attain anything of value in life — focus, effort and passionate persistence are needed.

No one is denied the drive towards
excellence — the wise one sees the
perfection of every outcome irrespective of
conventional evaluation and judgment.

Once you have made a choice you are not
free of the outcome, which may not fit fully
with what was hoped for.

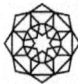

Do your best and leave the rest.

Whatever exists is never absolutely clear or
constant, but it has a touch of truth.

Deal with chaos in a neutral and insightful
way to discover order within it.

Don't deny darkness but seek the spark of
light within it which may lead you out of it.

Nature only reveals a minute amount of what is concealed. We cannot bear the immense range of the realities of nature via our mind, only the soul can.

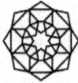

The perfumed rose began its journey in earth, water, and compost.

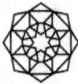

Whatever exists tends to continue.

Wars and poverty balance peace and wealth,
all of which are part of life's cycles and
changes.

The lioness is most gentle and loving with
her cubs but can instantly turn into a
vicious killer in defense or attack in order to
preserve life.

The middle way contains the extreme ends.

Confidence is due to a beam of light from
the soul. The arrogant ego-self also plays
its tricks with total trust; the outcome is
beyond confidence or lack of it.

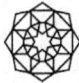

Whatever we consider as real through mind
and reason has only a touch of the Real.

You are always right and always wrong, at
the same time, always.

Our desire for good times is a precursor to experiencing the perfection of timelessness.

A good time is when you are relaxed and at ease; a better time when you lose all sense of time.

Most of the time you are purposeful but enjoy it more when you are relaxed with no concern or in deep sleep.

To change or transform the world, start with yourself and the process will become evolutionary and revolutionary at the same time.

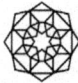

The ultimate freedom is liberation from the idea of freedom and living fully in the moment.

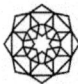

Your perspective on life and your values will change radically if you have only an hour to live.

Orphans

Insanity has many degrees of intensity and comes in two forms, one is mental and the other spiritual.

Certainty can follow doubt and vice versa.

7. Conduct

Total honesty, selflessness, and full
accountability in conduct are preparations for
higher consciousness.

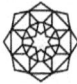

No one is spared a situation when one has
acted foolishly or lacked proper awareness.
The greater folly is to not reflect upon this
situation or simply deny or ignore it.

Your conduct belies your inner state as it
relates to the outer world.

To realise the presence of perfect governance of the universe, first practice optimum self-governance, honesty and accountability.

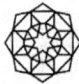

The state of your consciousness is revealed by your intention and actions.

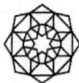

Self-importance is a perversion that conceals soul dominance or spiritual presence.

To do good at all times is a necessary concern for whoever strives for higher consciousness, which leads to a state where good and bad vanish into utter original perfection.

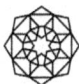

The desire for good reputation may lead to improved intentions and action or the pretense of goodness.

Goodness is only complete at the end of patience — just good without time limits.

In truth your conduct and behaviour is much worse than your critics accuse you of. And in truth within you is the perfect soul greater than anyone can ever describe.

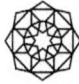

You may like or hate what the world brings to you. Admit your emotion and then read the situation as it is without your prejudice or judgment.

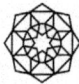

Generally, you like others to treat you with respect, love, dignity and honour, yet you often act or behave in a despicable position which deserves scorn.

When you reflect upon the absurd behaviour of people on earth you may feel like an alien.

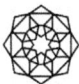

To damn anyone or any event is ignorance of one's own ignorance.

We are always wrong and yet in truth, there is nothing ever wrong.

The overall state of health and well-
being of a person's body, mind and soul
will determine the outcome of the day to
day interaction with the world outside.
Experiences are as good or bad as one's inner
and outer connection and relationship.

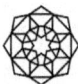

There is a primal drive to excel and improve
what we find — are you leaving the world
better than you found it?

Without the desire for outcomes, there will
be little earthly growth or improvements.

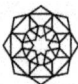

There is a primal drive to excel and improve
what we find — are you leaving the world
better than you found it?

The mischievous child tests boundaries
and conceals its wrong conduct. The young
adult may be more daring and can be
confrontational. The mature adult tries to
keep within the bounds to avoid disapproval.

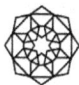

Sincerity and loyalty to what is local is the
beginning of sincerity to the universal.

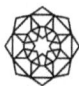

Even after proven wrong you still feel some
justification for what you did. Are you
infallible or is this behavior carrying traces
of the perfect soul?

Orphan

You were wrong this time. In truth you are
wrong every-time.

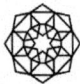

8. Consciousness, Connectivity and Continuity

What is experienced as real or true is a
glimpse of what is absolutely real and true.

Every living creature is driven to connect
with what is relevant for survival and
continuity to experience life.

Everything that expresses its state in
numerous ways, but the mind's natural
concern for survival filters out most of these
messages.

Body, mind, and emotions are the earthly
faculties that connect with our heavenly
origin of light — the soul.

Body, mind and self are transitions in
consciousness, energised by the soul and
supreme consciousness.

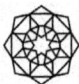

Pleasure is when you experience desirable
connectedness and its continuity, whereas
displeasure is due to undesirable connections
or discontinuity.

Reason and rationality are like ladders that
lead to the zone of pure consciousness that is
the source of life and all mental and sensory
experiences.

Wisdom is about context, relevance, balance
— appropriateness in time and place.

Wisdom starts with useful knowledge and
leads to beyond all differentiation and earthly
values.

You may get what you longed and dreamt for, but the next desire and hope may negate everything before.

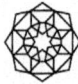

Celebrate achievement and certainty, but accept cheerfully the nature of our worldly experience with its constant uncertainty.

Even the greatest lie contains a spark of truth.

Normality means balance, reliability, and a combined state of change and constancy at the same time. Normal breathing is different from gasping for breath.

All constants, including scientific ones, are also relative but less than others.

Acting upon little wisdom is better than accumulating unused knowledge.

Wisdom, discernment and insights are a prelude to experiencing the ever-present conclusion — sacred light beyond mind, sight or self.

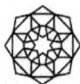

What we can measure and describe is only an aspect of what is immeasurable, defies definition, and is beyond mental comprehension.

If the earth is one year old, then humanity is twenty seconds old and the west rules for two seconds — reflect on this perspective.

Orphan

Worse than a lie is to deny it.
If you were in someone else's situation you
would do exactly as they did — right or
wrong.

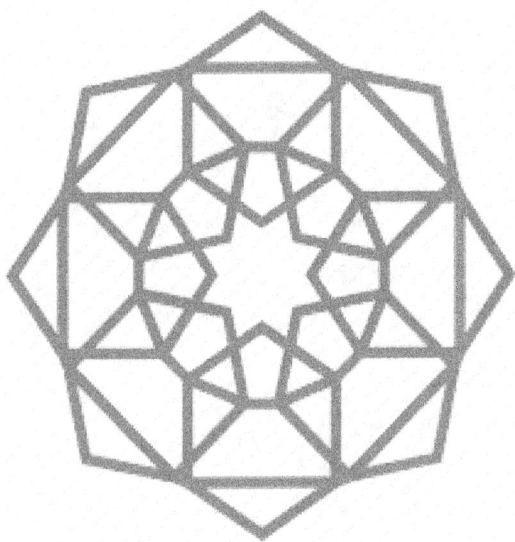

9. Polarity of Humanity

All humans are susceptible to fears, anxieties, sorrow and depression and other sufferings — mild or acute. This state can be transcended by the light of the soul within.

The dread and grace of difficulties is a natural conundrum and challenge to access higher consciousness.

Suffering is due to conditioned consciousness, which could open the path toward higher consciousness, or lead to doom and gloom.

To reduce future sorrow, guilt or suffering,
before any action, reflect upon the outcome
and potential unintended consequences.
Equally important, consider the way out of
such action with ease, as and when needed.

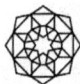

Guilt and regrets arise due to a lack of
presence when acting. These emotions do
not appear when one is fully present in mind
and heart.

Sorrow and grief are expressions of loss or
waste of opportunities for a better life.

The seed of insanity is nurtured by blame, claim and denial, due to the illusion of independent identity.

Blaming others and claiming superiority will stop when you discover the illusion of the independent self or a defined earthly role and identity.

Love and hate of self will only end when self has become One with soul.

Attachment is the cause of much suffering due to changes or uncertainties. It is also at the root of happiness when the attachment is to your soul.

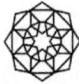

Due to desires and attachments, many human experiences are traps that cause suffering and the drive to be free from them. Then there are many other traps that await your fall.

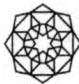

Human desire to win always brings about much suffering and occasionally may lead to the discovery of the ever-victorious Truth.

Everyone desires dignity, honor and respect
— all due to the glorious soul within.

Everyone is very ordinary but within the
heart lays the most extra-ordinary soul or
spirit.

'The other' may help to reduce some earthly
suffering; Oneness is the zone of perfect
bliss.

Who do you trust more than yourself? You are also likely to lose that trust — now where do you turn to other than the Truth itself.

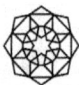

Most people behave and live in a dishonorable way, reflecting the lower ego-self.

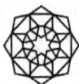

Misery, fear and sorrow are infestations that thrive in the darkness of the lower self.

It is natural for everything that exists in the
universe to disintegrate and be corrupted
except the original light of life — your soul
or spirit.

Darkness permeates every aspect of existence
and can only be dispelled when you
overcome your inner darkness of ego-self.

Discord and animosity will end when you are
guided by your divine soul.

Few people live fully in the NOW. Many fill
the moment with regret or sorrow about the
past and concern or fear of the future.

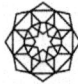

A better future is dependent on the extent
of the perfection of reading and living the
present.

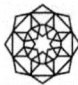

Whoever has harmed you also saved you
from being indebted to their goodness.

The lens of sadness is made of earthly dust
and happiness is from the light of the soul.

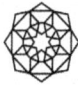

Fear, denial and anger regarding death is at
the level of conditioned consciousness and
does not exist with soul consciousness and
its continuity.

No expectation without suffering.

To see goodness in what is considered bad is
a step towards a higher state of consciousness
where good and bad merges into Oneness.

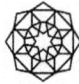

Lasting happiness is due to the acceptance
of the present moment and being
at one with it.

It is a great fortune to be content at heart
and cheerfully balanced during ease as well as
difficulties.

Orphan

Expectations distort reading of facts and reality.

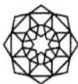

10. Differentiated Sameness

In their essential nature, all humans are the same, and different outwardly at all times.

Dualities and change are the nature of existence emanating from the constant and perfect source of the oneness.

When a difference is investigated fully to its origin, it reveals sameness.

Respect for passing shadows in creation
simply acknowledges the grace of the light
which is the source of creation and life.

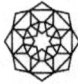

Most people seek variety, choice and
diversity; very few seek the hidden thrills of
singularity and cosmic unity, the essence of
differentiated sameness.

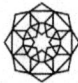

Everything in existence is interdependent
as discerned by our consciousness
— which itself is dependent upon Supreme
Consciousness.

We strive to be independent and self-reliant
and yet we are totally dependent upon life's
mysterious source with countless other
factors such as air, water and material objects
and energies.

The pursuit of independence will inevitably
lead to a dead end. Life is experienced
within universal interdependence.

Dependently interdependent is the state of
every living creature.

Whatever you are aware of or know is a passing shadow, and your perpetual desire and quest are to know the original cause of all lights and shadows.

Whatever exists reveals an aspect of temporary reality that emanates from what is Real.

All experiences are within dualities, originating and returning to unity.

At the beginning of an event, you may have hints about its outcome. Everything is interconnected in creation without us being fully aware of these links within time.

All experiences are within dualities, originating and returning to unity.

As creatures of habit, we like the same experience with slight modification — or new experience with some connection to the past.

Close friends experience love and oneness
and enemies exchange repulsion, aggression
and destruction. One lot moves towards
unity and the other to dispersion and loss.

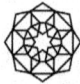

Without others, you may not survive and
with others, you are challenged to connect in
appropriate ways.

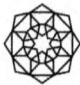

Love and knowledge unite, hatred and
ignorance divide.

To understand another person's behaviour,
you need to put yourself fully in their
position.

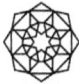

If you manage to put yourself fully in
someone else's position, you will behave
exactly as they do. This is the basis of full
understanding, compassion and forgiveness.

When you love someone you empathise
to the extent you feel their state, concerns
and hopes. Instead of one person caught in
emotional turmoil, now there are two.

To experience unconditional love and closeness with another human being is an earthly sample of lasting unity and cosmic oneness.

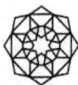

To be in love is to flow along the unifying field of love and experience a touch of Oneness.

The mind is like a web that connects heavenly energies with earthly entities.

Belief in oneself is a factor for outer success;
knowledge of the nature of the soul is the
source of enlightenment.

Whomever you regard as an enemy is only
the dark shadow of a potential friend.

True prophets and enlightened beings are
veiled behind the mist of lights and shadows.

Durable contentment is the outcome
of understanding the different levels of
realities, dualities, unity, the spectrum of
consciousness and the rise of conditioned
consciousness because of the confinement
within space and, time which emerged from
boundlessness and, returns to it.

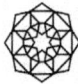

Dualities and pluralities are messengers of
unity.

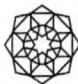

Diversity is a temporary veil of singularity.

The ultimate challenge and
purpose of human life is to witness
unity in all dualities.

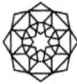

Don't fully trust anything that is definable,
any solid can become fluid or gas.

11. Beyond Time

To experience infinity, you need infinite
speed or the ability to stop time.

Every fleeting moment carries a veil of
timelessness.

Pleasure makes time and distance appear
shorter.

Lasting joy does not exist in the
confinement of space or time where
everything is transitory.

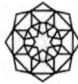

Fear and ignorance live within time, and
truth declares there is no time.

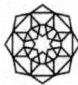

The moment was, is and will be
ever-constant and ever-moving
at the same time.

When you lose all concepts of time people
may consider you mad and you, in turn,
wonder about the sanity of those confused
between past, present and future.

Your future is here and now, and yet it seems
absent.

Now is better than any other time, even
better than what is considered beyond time.

Every moment is sacred and so is every place,
all have emerged from the sacred origin.

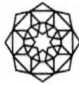

When you know you have much time
available, you cannot waste a minute.

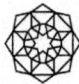

The young are in a rush and the old are
slow, yet time flows constantly.

The present moment is often lost between
the past and future.

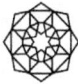

Sorrow and regrets are due to past mistakes,
whereas most fears and concerns are due
to future uncertainties and that is how the
present moment slips away.

Don't miss this moment in your life, you
can't catch it nor stop it, just flow with it.

12. Inner Compass

The human journey is in three stages:
the first is birth, the second is growth in
consciousness towards awakening, and the
third is the journey of the soul after death.

To find your way more easily in your earthly
journey you need to refer to your inner
spiritual compass.

An appropriate prescription may lead to
a clear understanding and acceptance of a
situation. Your life on earth is like being in a
waiting room expecting to be called to your
destination of pure consciousness.

The drive towards excellence and perfection
is a primary force in us, reflecting the
perfect soul within.

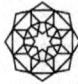

It is a natural drive to be in pursuit of real
identity and purpose of life.

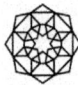

An important social drive is to be useful,
accepted, and acknowledged by others.

The Master said, "It is not what I have that attracts you to me, it is more what I don't have: I don't have the concerns, fears and desires you all have."

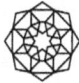

No person can help you realise the truth but may be helpful to remove some falsehood and ignorance. Truth reveals itself by itself when the recipient is ready.

You always hope to find someone you can totally rely upon, to love and die for, that is your own soul.

To see one object clearly you need two eyes.
To realise truth, you also need one clear head
and a pure unattached heart.

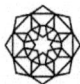

You may read the situation more clearly
after you lose all your ambitions and other
illusions.

An event or story is complete only when it
ends.

The personal life of the seeker of truth is
enhanced by remembering death.

'To forget' is balanced by 'to remember'.

The heart knows, but what do we know of
the heart and how it knows?

Most of us will naturally experience
loneliness until we fully embrace our inner
soul.

Loneliness is a primal desire to be at one
with the soul, the real union.

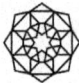

You are fortunate if you reach a point where
you really don't know who you are, with your
mind and intellect intact.

We often welcome what is new, provided it does not displace a cherished old value or object unless it brings greater benefits.

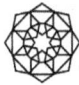

Surprise is what is not expected; we like the surprise that enhances life and dislike what increases fear and suffering.

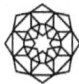

There will always be something that we miss, yet we don't want to miss anything considered good.

Leisure and pleasure often may lead to
degrading consciousness, unless there is
conscious effort to transcend mind and
senses.

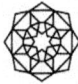

Whenever you think you have some extra
space or time, they often get filled up with
waste material.

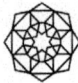

Your fate follows your choice.

There is no option in desiring options or in hoping to choose the appropriate one.

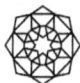

All deception or falsehood contains a spark of truth.

The flip side of an inferior state can be a superior one, imagined or real.

The self enjoys power, wealth,
acknowledgment, respect, status, control,
victory, achievement, success, constancy,
highest beauty, ease, comfort, luxury, pomp,
ceremony, admiration and adoration.

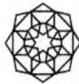

The self is never wrong, instant gratification,
desirable, contentment, free to do anything
anytime, access to any knowledge desired.

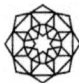

The self loves to be considered generous,
fair, correct, compassionate, patient,
knowing, forgiving, trusting, and
courageous.

If you believe in a supreme and just God,
then you accept whatever has affected you as
it could only happen with God's approval.

Self-image, self-esteem, and prestige are
important for the young but can be an
obstacle and a handicap for mature seekers
of truth.

The ultimate spiritual challenge is to
transcend the mind and realise that two plus
two is still One.

Orphan

You experience super confidence when you have gone past the illusion of self-confidence.

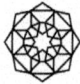

13. Teachers and Teachings

The extent and truth regarding the state of a spiritual teacher is an important consideration. Consciousness flows from a base level of sentiency toward pure consciousness. Many spiritual teachers and seekers may have had a touch of the high voltage of pure consciousness for a short while or longer. The movement is from self-ego consciousness to soul presence or pure consciousness.

When the teacher is predominantly within the soul zone, then the ego-self interference is minimum, though it is still there, especially if there is interaction with other creation. The lower self-consciousness is at its minimum when there is a severance of interaction, such as being in seclusion.

You can assess the extent of the person's state of consciousness if you observe what they say or do. A higher state of awakening is accompanied by, amongst others, the following:

- Unaffected by praise or censure of others.
- Mostly unaffected by good or bad news.
- The least extent of ambition, desires, or attachments.
- No fears, sorrows or any suffering.
- Physical illness or pain is regarded as a natural fact without emotional or inner suffering or regrets.
- Fully in the present without being much influenced by the past or concern about the future.

Empathy or sympathy with others is genuine at the time but is not internalised resulting in a negative in the mind.

No denial of personal needs for survival or for leading a quality life but is not emotionally affected by deficiencies.

    i. Regards outer loss as an opportunity

for outer improvement as well as a spring for inner growth in higher consciousness.

ii. Regards death as a release of the soul to experience a new state of life without confusion and darkness.

When the teacher is not fully enlightened, the spiritual discourse is prolonged and vague.

14. Religion and Culture

Religion thrives within cultures and like a
plant grows and withers according to the
quality of soil and care. A living religion
needs a living soul.

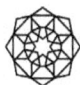

The earthly side of our nature has evolved
from the beginning of creation and relates
to all that exists. Religious practices and
disciplines may help to focus on the source
of our origin.

When the sense of the sacred is lost in a
culture, that culture is about to be lost.

There is no need to change your religion.
If you are obsessed with cosmic light and
resonate with it, then humanity and divinity
are in resonance.

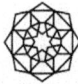

If you learned to follow the light of your
own soul, you would not be confused about
different religions, paths or authentic
teachers or gurus. Your guidance emanates
from your own heart.

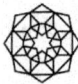

Religion and culture of the rulers or
colonialists dominate upon the inhabitants'
old ways.

More conflicts, wars and sorrow occur
due to ideas, beliefs and hopes than factual
dangers or real threats to life.

Most religious people talk about happiness
rather than being happy, and that is why
they become intolerant and dogmatic.

Religious or spiritual paths intend to
lift ordinary consciousness to a higher
level however it is the nature of limited
conditioned consciousness to resist due to
the attachment of its illusion of security.

When your belief, ideology or religion has not delivered what was promised, you look for outer enemies and causes of failure other than yourself.

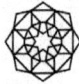

15. Higher Consciousness

Human drives and hopes are towards higher
consciousness when viewed with insight and
reflection.

Without the experiences of higher
consciousness and the thrill of Oneness,
divisions and discord will poison one's life.

A neutral attitude towards the unknown will
lead to the door of higher consciousness.

Success and failure are common human
experiences whereas lasting victory
belongs to higher consciousness and its
boundlessness.

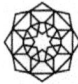

Most obsessions are obstructions to higher
consciousness except the obsession for
higher consciousness itself.

The human quest for the permanent is the
drive that will reveal eternal life.

Basic intelligence connects stimulus-response and causality. Other numerous levels of intelligence lead to the highest and subtlest of lights and spiritual consciousness which, when confused and jumbled, cause insanity.

When limited conditioned consciousness connects with full consciousness lasting grace and contentment are experienced.

To be content and balanced is a necessary state to experience higher consciousness.

The natural tendency to fill your space and time is the distraction from the experience of higher consciousness.

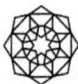

Boredom is due to the lack of a stimulus or a flow of continuity towards higher consciousness.

Change is due to consciousness experiencing a new connection, sometimes imperceptible.

Creativity, art and music expand
consciousness and can bring about feelings
of well-beingness, especially when the ego
and self-concern are lessened.

Habits are important for ease of flow in
outer life and breaking of habits can increase
openings and insights to truth and higher
consciousness.

Eating is creative destruction and so is
turning against the ego.

What you dislike may be of greater benefit to your growth in consciousness than that which you like.

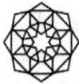

Outer clearing is to give away what is not needed, and inner clearing is to give away that which you want to keep.

More is more in mental measures, and less is more along the spiritual ladder.

Your quality of life will increase as you
journey toward higher consciousness.

Higher consciousness reduces suffering and
concerns about physical limitations.

Perspective is like the two long poles that
hold the ladder of consciousness.

Higher consciousness will remain obscure to those in a superficial state of comfort and ease. Unless the ego is challenged, the light of the soul will not prevail.

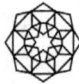

With old age, you lose much of youthful desires and drives which may be replaced with access to higher consciousness and awakening to Truth.

To love another may be the first step to be at one with the One, with no other.

Orphan

Facts are the background of realities
illumined by Truth.

16. Witnessing Perfection

When witnessing occurs due to the absence
of the witness's identity and values, only
perfect witnessing is the outcome.

The illusion of personal will and choice
drives the ego-self to evolve and realise the
truth that higher consciousness ends choice
and leads to the experience of perfection
perpetually.

Occasionally you may marvel at excellence or
perfection. Some other times you experience
frustration or disappointment at failure or
loss. When you experience the ever-presence
of grace you are not afflicted by good or bad.

All earthly experiences of beauty and perfection conceal a fault and blemish to remind us of the temporary and imperfect nature of our earthly experiences.

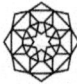

Natural beauty and majesty appear on the surface of a multitude of entities and events.

Intelligence drives you to change the world and then to change yourself and then to witness perfections in all that changes and that which does not.

Lasting contentment occurs when earthly
well-beingness and security are due to
witnessing the perfection of cosmic Reality
and its governance.

Earthly gardens are a metaphor of paradise:
a state of harmony, and beauty in forms,
fragrance and magic of life.

Joy is a gift of grace and can increase with
heartfelt gratitude.

Orphan

We want the latest and we want it now, for
truth is ever-fresh and ever-present.

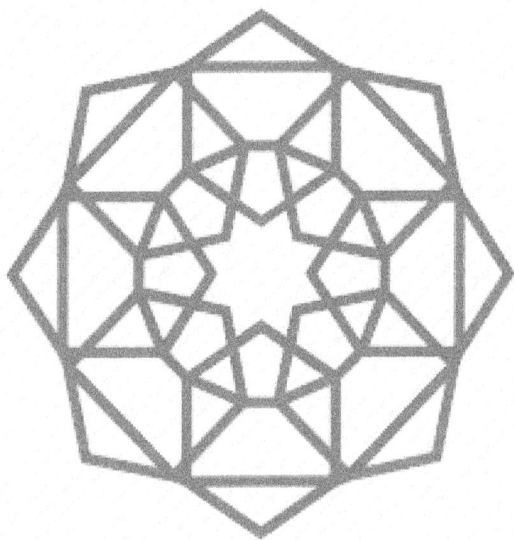

17. Destiny

The best destiny is to be with eternal
Oneness.

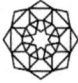

Human consciousness is temporary, limited
and conditioned, whereas its origin and
destiny are eternal pure consciousness.

Destiny and origin are twins that reside in
timeless infinity.

Destiny is ever perfect irrespective of
personal judgment and experience.

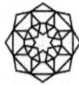

Real acceptance of the moment enables you
to flow with ease along your destiny.

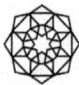

Pain prolongs time. What makes distance
long is strong emotion and the need to get
to your destiny.

18. Reality

God decides everything without being
affected by anything and that decision
incorporates the hopes and wills of
all living creatures.

All of creation is driven by the Truth, God
or the Divine Creator towards realising its
glorious immensity.

Truth is ever-constant and ever-
present irrespective of our embracing or
denouncing it.

Truth and reality are ever constant and permanent. Everything that exists and all experiences are temporary but carry within them a spark of the permanent truth.

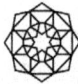

Wherever you look Truth beams. Like looking at direct sunlight you don't see anything unless you reduce the light's intensity — we only understand when there is both truth and some falsehood.

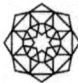

Truth and Reality have no end as they are not confined to space and time (whereas) falsehood and illusions will always come to an end.

When the sun of truth appears in your sky
all the millions of stars fade away. When
cosmic reality shines all other values and
ideas vanish.

Truth is experienced when all other notions,
ideas or thoughts have ended.

Progress towards the Real begins by
recognising what is not real.

Everything in life can be discussed, analysed and evaluated except TRUTH: It is due to it that we differentiate and understand.

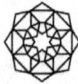

Truth is beyond the reach of rationality and reason and is the cause of all mental processes.

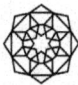

We look for truth within facts. In truth, facts are basic indicators of truth.

In truth there is only Truth. The seeker and sought are in the shadows of Truth.

To touch the boundary of Reality you need to leave the experience of duality.

On earth, there is no absolute freedom. In heavens, there is no freedom or lack of it.

All our experiences and discoveries are steps towards the ultimate reality and Truth.

Changing identity and crises in life may be preludes to experiencing Reality.

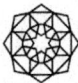

Every instant is real in its connection to the Ever-real.

Harmony and bliss surround the light of
sacredness which is the source of life and
consciousness.

Truth is in absolute perfect balance and,
in our relative and changing world, all
imbalances are short-lived.

Universal changing diversity is balanced by
original cosmic constant unity.

The greatest discovery is that Truth is the only True Reality and the greatest victory is to be at one with Truth.

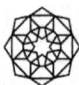

The cosmic reality is perpetual and constant — from it, all varieties, temporary and virtual appearances emanate and then vanish back to it.

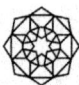

God's house has no doors or walls. It is the boundless universe.

19. Awakening

Awakening to Truth is a state that
envelops you as a result of being at
one with the One.

Spiritual awakening erases the rational,
logical and balanced reason. Higher
consciousness is a unitive zone that has no
separations or differentiations — absolute
Oneness.

The most valuable thing in existence is to
know that life is the ultimate treasure and to
yield to its origin is the nature of awakening,
a gift beyond measure.

To realise the ultimate treasure of reality itself you need to give up all other values and interests so as to transcend all shadows of reality to Truth itself.

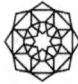

Live in trust of the One, respond by permission of the One, and see through the light of the One.

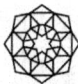

The light of Truth shines when personal life merges with eternal life itself.

You are not who you think you are. When all shadows disappear and only the original light remains; this is your reality and true identity.

The widest gap in the universe is the distance between losing oneself and finding it in the soul.

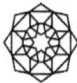

The root of betrayal is the denial of the soul or higher consciousness which is the origin and source of life itself. All other denials and discord are due to the lack of acknowledgement of this truth.

There is liberation in leaving all thoughts
behind and experiencing the infinitude of
the perpetual NOW.

Awakening is the result of giving up desires
and fear of outcomes.

Spiritual insights may follow when you lose
sight of yourself.

The extent of spiritual awakening is according to the relationship with life and death, and the knowledge that death is the ultimate gift to realise perpetual life.

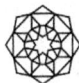

Birth and death are the expressions of manifest and hidden life.

Death is not the end of your life. It is when your soul leaves its temporary residence to return to the eternal abode. Death is the beginning of a new experience in life.

The awakened being sees the folly of others
who cause their own tragedies and dramas,
his heart's smile at this insight is balanced by
a touch of human empathy for those afflicted
with the darkness of the self.

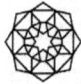

Awakening to truth removes the fear of
death and brings about total connectedness
and reverence for eternal life itself.

Ordinary folks grieve and fear death
whereas the awakened being rejoices in
the knowledge that there is perfection in
whatever exists.

You will experience the perfect grace of life
after befriending death.

When the relationship with death changes
from fear to friendship, higher consciousness
prevails over lower states.

Human life is a relentless practice of
reconciling with death and the end of
personal life.

Death is a natural event and will be experienced cheerfully when you know your soul is ever-living.

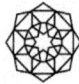

Whatever is within time and space will be lost and forgotten. Original light is ever constant and not subject to renewal, balance or forgetfulness.

A story is complete when it ends and you will know the full story of your life with the experience of death, before or after the biological end.

Sleep is at the foundation of human consciousness and is at the root of all states of awareness, such as the waking state, dreams, imagination as well as self and soul.

Every minute you are different and yet you consider yourself to be the same self.

Without memory, connections and continuity will be disrupted, yet memory is one of the veils of Reality.

Alchemy is transformation to grace,
which reveals cosmic realities and their
boundlessness at every moment and
situation.

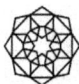

The drive for the limitless is a natural
response to the Truth that human life is a
sample of the cosmic Reality beyond space
or time as well as its source.

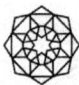

The extent of awakening to the Real
relates to the extent of the consistency of
experiencing Divine Grace.

You may appear cheerful by avoiding the big
question in life, its purpose and outcome.
The real happy person is alive fully in the
vastness of now, where there are no fears or
sorrows, perfect contentment in the present
now.

The root of selfishness is to preserve and
prolong life and the root of selflessness is to
lose the shadow self to the eternal soul.

An ordinary person's interest in eternal truth
is like a sleepwalker, expecting water in a
desert. The awakened sees by the light of
Truth and manages by effort and grace to
leave.

Most peoples' actions are based on short-term interest and need. The awakened ones act for posterity and perpetuity guided by Truth.

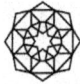

The desire for enlightenment may cause you to go beyond rational behaviour and other constraints.

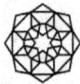

The shaman hunter became his prey, the seeker will lose identity and sense of purpose.

Presence in the moment is being fully
connected with all that exists.

Our tendency to cut corners or get there
sooner reflects that whatever we seek is
already here within the perfectly contented
soul within.

The constant drive to improve on any
situation will only stop with the experience
of the perfect moment, as every moment is.

When you are fully in the moment you only witness perfections, as all hopes, fears and other emotions vanish into timelessness.

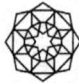

The young rush and fast forward time, the old are slow in motion, and the awakened experience time as a shadow emerging from timelessness.

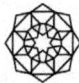

The best time and place is here and now.

What a difference between personal desire
and pursuit of power and to flow along with
cosmic power.

An activity flows with greater ease when
your self is in harmony with your soul.

Actions may help with learning and wisdom
but are redundant when you are at one with
your soul.

The quest for perfection leads to the
presence of perfection NOW.

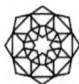

After connecting to the event and experience
of its perfections, be thrilled as to how the
unseen directs the tangible experience.

It is an enlightened moment when you
experience the total perfection of the
moment.

Real gnosis is the realisation and trust
that the present moment reveals the truth,
according to one's ability to accept it.

For Plato and Aristotle, knowledge of the
eternal and of truth lie where words end.

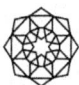

Your heart is your inner mirror that reflects
the truth, which the self may be opposed to.

The value of a secret is as good as the extent of its concealment. Once it is known, it loses its power. God remains as the absolute secret.

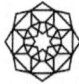

Human secrets are worthless while divine secrets reveal themselves according to perfect divine patterns of connectedness.

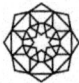

Truth enables you to access a state beyond contentment or misery. It is the essence of your own soul.

Celebration is only worthy of the Real, true,
constant and permanent, within everything
and at all times.

'Look what I got' is the declaration of
temporary success. 'Look what has got me'
is the celebration of whoever is awakened to
boundless consciousness.

You think you have got it but in truth,
it has got you.